MAGICAL
PANCHATANTRA STORIES

Magical Panchatantra Stories
ISBN : 978-93-5049-422-6

Reprinted in 2012

Published by :

SHREE BOOK CENTRE
8, Kakad Indl Estate, S. Keer Marg, Matunga West,
Mumbai - 400016, INDIA.
Phone : 91-22-24377516 / 24374559
Telefax : 91-22-24309183
E-mail : sales@shreebookcentre.com

© Shree Book Centre
No part of this publication may be reproduced, stored in or introduced into retrieval system transmitted in any form by any means (Electronic, Mechanical, Photocopying, recording, internet or otherwise) without prior written permission of the copyright owner.

Printed in India

Preface

The Panchatantra, as the name suggests, was originally a collection of five volumes of stories written in Sanskrit by a wise pundit named Vishnu Sharman in the 3rd century BC. It is believed that these stories were for the benefit of three ignorant princes to teach them lessons in the wise conduct of life.

The stories have been told and retold over generations and are, today, the most frequently translated Indian work into foreign and Indian languages. The stories teach valuable lessons in life through vivid tales of characters from the animal kingdom. Children will be simply delighted as crows and owls talk about friendship and trust, monkeys and jackals about equality and success, and fishes and frogs about greed and honesty.

Narrated in simple language and printed in large print with attractive illustrations on each page, these books are simply be delightful from start to finish. The glossary at the end of the book with meanings of difficult words will add to your child's vocabulary.

Give these enchanting books to your child.

CONTENTS

1. The Lion and the Talking Cave — 1
2. The Owl and the Swan — 9
3. The Fox and the Grapes — 17
4. The Brahmin and His Foolish Sons — 25
5. The Tree That Talked — 33
6. The Brahmin and His Dream — 41
7. The Cap Seller and the Monkeys — 49
8. The Crow and the Jackal — 57
9. The Crane and the Crab — 65

The Lion and the Talking Cave

Once upon a time, a clever jackal made his home in a cave in the forest. Every day, he would leave the cave at sunrise in search of food, and return at sunset.

In the same forest lived a lion. He had grown very old and could no longer run fast to catch his prey. Because of this, he often had to go hungry.

One day, the Lion tried to catch a lame deer. But, even the lame deer could run faster than him!

As the lion wandered in search of a prey, he saw the jackal's cave. He was sure that some animal lived in the cave. He had an idea! He went into the cave.

The lion waited inside the cave for the whole day. He was very hungry and this made him very restless and impatient.

At sunset, the jackal came back to find the forest quiet around the cave. There were lion's pug marks leading to the cave, but not coming out. The clever jackal was sure that some great danger lurked inside the cave. He thought of a plan and called out to the cave.

The jackal was only pretending to talk to the cave. But the lion was taken in. He believed that the cave was in the habit of speaking to the jackal, asking him in! As the cave did not seem to be doing so today, the hungry lion in his haste decided to call out on its behalf!

"Tchah! How could I be so foolish! Now I've lost my prey!"

He roared. The jackal at once recognised the roar and was sure there was a lion in his cave. He turned and ran for his life.

The lion waited for the jackal to come in but soon realised that he had been fooled. He left the cave, hungry and disappointed. The clever jackal had been watching from a safe distance. He waited till the lion was out of sight and then returned to the cave for a good night's rest.

Moral: Haste is at the bottom of all mistakes.

The Owl and the Swan

A swan and an owl once lived in the jungle. They were good friends. The swan was the king of swans, but the owl was just a common bird.

One day, the owl woke up to see an army camp beneath his tree. Suddenly, he had an idea! He quickly went to the swan and invited him to his tree.

Just then, the captain gave the orders to the army to move. Hearing this, the owl decided to show the swan his authority. He flew around the captain hooting loudly.

Now, the captain was a man who believed in omens. He quickly decided that it was not a good day to travel. So, the captain cancelled his orders and the army remained there.

The next morning, the owl again invited the swan to show off his kingdom. As the soldiers were getting ready to go, the owl flew around the captain's head hooting loudly.

But, this time, the captain was angry with the owl. He decided that he would set aside his fear of ill omens and continue with the journey. He called an archer.

The owl and the swan were perched on the same branch when the archer shot his arrow. The owl seeing the arrow, moved away hastily. But the swan was too slow to move...

The owl was filled with sadness and remorse at the loss of the noble swan. If he had not been so untruthful and vain, he would not have caused the death of a good and honest friend.

Moral: Disaster follows pride.

The Fox and the Grapes

Once, there lived a fox in a forest. He had not eaten for many days. He felt very hungry and weak and longed to find something to eat.

As the fox wandered around, searching for food, he came to a village at the edge of the forest. There he saw a vineyard. There were big bunches of ripe grapes hanging from the vines.

The fox looked around to see if anyone from the village was around. There was no one in sight. He squeezed himself through a hole in the hedge and entered the vineyard.

Not having eaten for many days, the poor fox feasted his eyes on the ripe, delicious-looking grapes. But, he soon realised that they were quite high.

The fox jumped up with his mouth wide open to snap up a big bunch of grapes, but they were just beyond his reach and his mouth closed over the thin air!

The hungry fox did not give up. The sight of the ripe, juicy grapes was too much for him. He moved back a few paces so that he could run and jump higher.

> Grrr. Fall you wretched grapes. Can't you see I'm hungry?

But, the fox just could not jump high enough to reach the grapes! He was hungry and tired. Angry now, he caught hold of the poles holding up the vines and tried to shake them.

Even that did not work. At last, the fox gave up and turned to leave. As he was going, he took one last look at the grapes hanging on the vines, and said, "Oh! Never mind! I am sure the grapes are sour!"

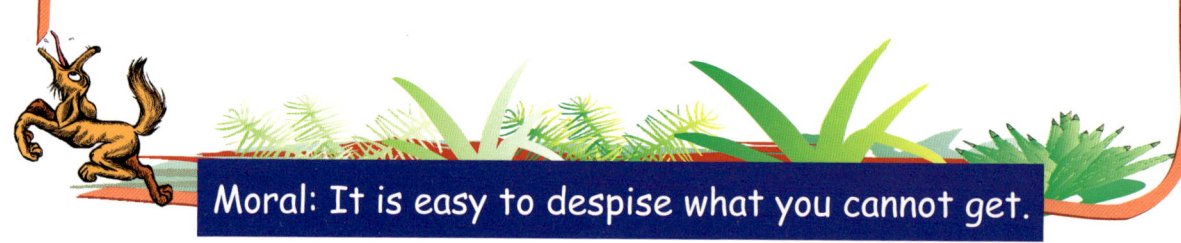

Moral: It is easy to despise what you cannot get.

The Brahmin and His Foolish Sons

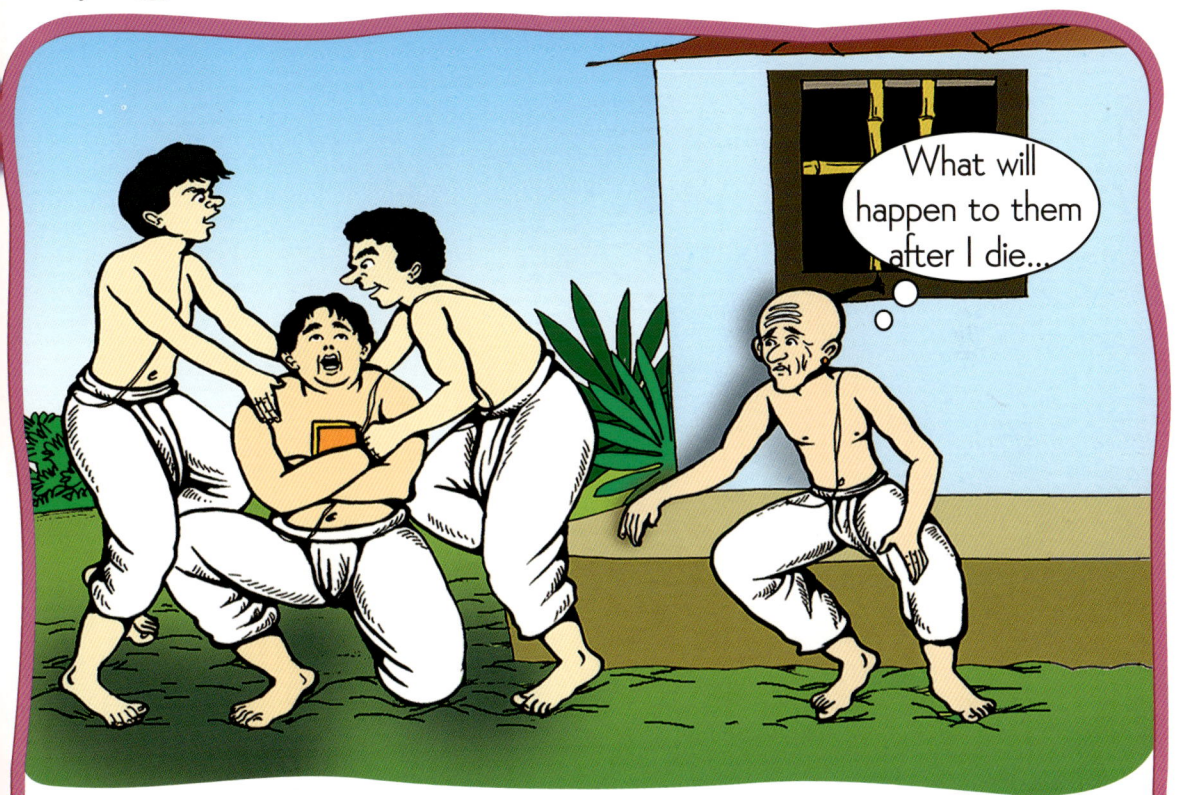

Once upon a time, there lived an old and wise Brahmin. But the Brahmin's three sons were very foolish. They spent all their time quarrelling. The old Brahmin was very worried for them.

After thinking for many days, the Brahmin hit upon a good plan. He called his three sons together. He handed a short stick to each of them, and asked them to break the sticks. All three of them broke the sticks easily.

The wise old Brahmin had known that his young sons would find it easy to break the single sticks. Now, as they watched curiously, he took three similar sticks and tied them together.

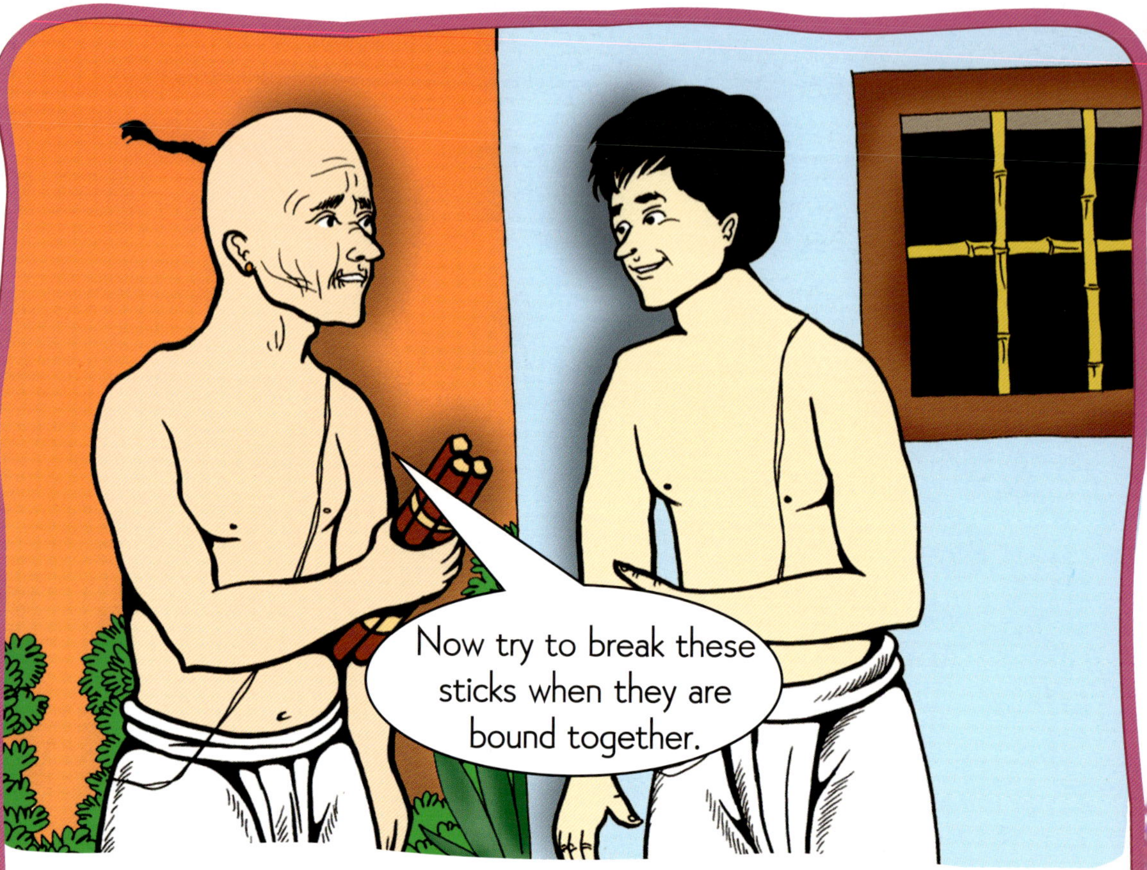

The wise Brahmin then called his eldest son and handed the three sticks bound together, and asked him to try to break it.

Let me see if you can break the three sticks.

When the eldest son could not break the three sticks bound together, the old Brahmin called his second son and asked him to try to break the bundle of sticks.

When even the second son could not break the bundle, the Brahmin called his youngest son and asked him to see if he could succeed at what his two elder brothers had failed to do.

"Even when all of us try, we are not able to break these sticks when they are together!"

When none of them could break the bundle, the old Brahmin asked them to collectively try to break the three sticks bound together.

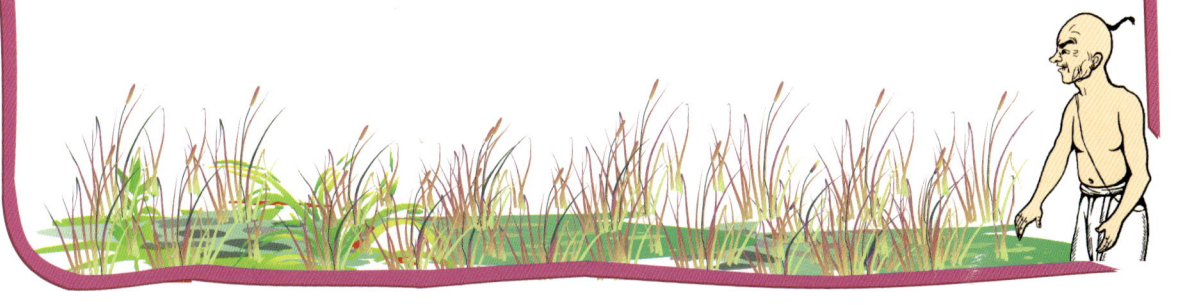

"You see my sons, unity is true strength!"

They failed.

When the brothers saw that they could not break the sticks, which were tied into a bundle, they realised what their father was trying to teach them – only if they were united, would they be strong enough to face life's difficulties.

Moral: United we stand, divided we fall.

The Tree That Talked

This is a good place for us to rest tonight.

Once, two friends, Papabuddhi and Dharmabuddhi were travelling through a forest. They were going back home after selling their goods in a nearby town. All their money was in one bag.

As darkness was falling, they decided to rest. Papabuddhi was a very dishonest person and decided to cheat his friend of all the money. So, he sat up hatching a plot while Dharmabuddhi rested.

The next day, Papabuddhi told Dharmabuddhi that it might not be safe to travel with so much money. They should bury the money under a tree for safe keeping. Dharmabuddhi agreed.

"Now I can have all this money to myself!"

Soon, the two friends were back home in their village. But that night, Papabuddhi came back alone and dug out the bag and took away all the money.

"You thief, you stole all our money. I'm going to the village elders for justice."

The following day, the two friends went back to dig out the money, and found that it had been stolen.

Papabuddhi immediately accused his poor friend of the theft.

"The tree is my witness. Let us go and ask the tree spirit."

They went to the village elders. Papabuddhi insisted that Dharmabuddhi had stolen the money. He even said that he had the tree spirit as a witness. The tree would talk and tell people that it was Dharmabuddhi who was to be blamed for the theft! Hearing this, Dharmabuddhi understood that it was all a plot of his wicked friend.

"Truly, the tree spirit has spoken. You are guilty."

So, they all went to the tree that would talk. This, too, was part of Papabuddhi's plan. He had asked his old father to hide in the hollow trunk of the tree. Sure enough, everybody heard a voice in the tree saying that Dharmabuddhi had indeed stolen the money. The elders believed the voice to come from the tree spirit and also believed that it spoke the truth!

Cough! It is all my dishonest son's fault. He is the one who stole all the money. Gasp!

But as they were talking, Dharmabuddhi, who was not only honest but also clever, picked up some dry leaves and lit a fire under the tree trunk. In a short while, the old father jumped out coughing, because of the smoke, and accepted his son's guilt.

Moral: The greedy never prosper.

The Brahmin and His Dream

Please accept this and bless my home O holy one!

There once lived a poor Brahmin. He was a priest in a small temple, and lived on the alms given by the people of the town he lived in. One day, a pious lady gave him a generous measure of wheat flour.

The Brahmin was very happy. He went home and poured the flour into an earthen pot and placed it at the foot of his cot. He then lay down and began to daydream.

The Brahmin dreamt that he had sold the flour and bought a goat.

He further dreamt that he made so much money with his goat that he bought a cow.

"Now that I have a house, it's time to marry."

The poor Brahmin dreamed on. He dreamt that he had become so rich selling the cow's milk that he bought himself a big house.

Now that I am married, we will have a son.

The Brahmin's dream seemed most real to him. He now dreamt that he got married to the beautiful daughter of a rich merchant.

"I want you to take good care of our son."

In the Brahmin's dream, a son was born to him. He was proud that he was the father of a beautiful son.

But, his wife was not taking good care of their son! He was so angry with this that he gave her a kick.

Alas! Because of my day dreaming, I knocked down the flour. Now I have nothing to eat.

The Brahmin kicked his leg in his dream. He suddenly awoke to a loud crash. He had kicked the pot of flour and the flour had scattered all over the floor!

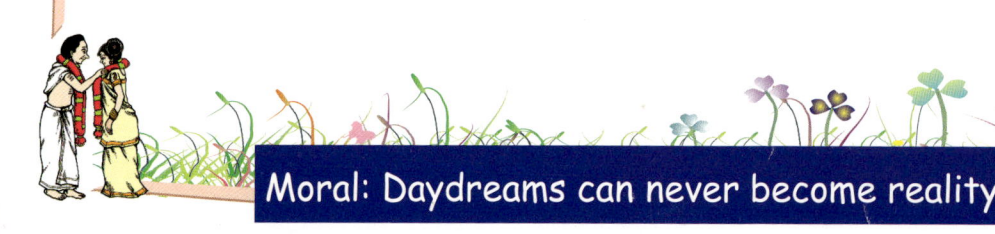

Moral: Daydreams can never become reality.

The Cap Seller and the Monkeys

There was once a cap seller, who sold caps in different towns and villages. Each day, he travelled a long way on foot, carrying a huge basket full of caps. One hot day, he was crossing the woods. He was very tired and needed some rest.

He put his heavy basket aside and lay down. The poor cap seller was so tired that the next moment he fell fast asleep.

As he lay sleeping, a group of monkeys, that lived in the forest, came down from the trees. They were attracted by the colourful caps, and started playing with them.

Suddenly, the cap seller woke up with a start. He was shocked to see the monkeys playing with his caps. Seeing him awake, the monkeys scampered up the trees with the caps.

The cap seller was very angry when he saw that the monkeys had snatched his caps. He pointed his finger at them and shouted angrily. The monkeys immediately imitated him.

The cap seller was a clever man. He realised that the monkeys would imitate whatever he did. He had an idea. He took a cap and wore it on his head. The monkeys immediately did the same with the caps they had snatched from him.

"Good! My plan has worked. I can now get my caps back."

The clever cap seller then took the cap off his head and threw it on the ground. Seeing him, the monkeys did the same with the caps on their heads!

> If I hurry I can get to the next village before nightfall.

The clever cap seller gathered all the caps the monkeys had thrown down and put them back into his basket. Then, he put the basket on his head and went on his way to the next village.

Moral: Wisdom always prevails over foolishness.

The Crow and the Jackal

Once, a crow saw an old Brahmin eating some bread. The crow was very hungry. When the Brahmin was looking away, she quickly snatched a piece of bread and flew away with it.

The hungry crow flew away to a tree in the woods nearby and sat down to eat the tasty piece of bread.

Just then, a jackal came up from behind. He saw the crow sitting on the tree with the bread in her beak. The jackal was a very cunning and greedy animal.

"O beautiful bird, are you new to the woods? I have never seen another bird as pretty as you!"

He wanted to take the bread away from the crow and eat it himself. He thought fast and came up with a plan. He went over to the crow and started praising her.

At first, the crow ignored the jackal. She knew that the jackal was a cunning animal. But the jackal did not give up. He praised her even more. "Your black feathers have a special shine today!" he said.

The crow began to feel flattered. She had never heard so many nice things being said about her. She even started believing in the jackal's words. "A beautiful bird like you surely has a beautiful voice too!" the jackal continued.

The crow listened to the jackal's words of flattery and believed that she could sing. She decided to sing! Just as she opened her beak to sing, the bread fell down from her beak – only to be snapped up by the cunning jackal!

It was then that the poor crow realised that the jackal had tricked her. As she looked down helplessly, the jackal went away with the piece of bread.

Moral: Flattery is the weapon of the cunning.

The Crane and the Crab

One day, in the forest, a crane stood at the edge of a pond looking sad and thoughtful. But, in his mind he had a wicked plan.

The fishes of the pond felt sorry when they saw the crane looking so sad. They asked him the reason for his sadness. The crane told them that he was blessed and that he could see into the future. "The future of the fishes in this pond is very sad, as the pond is going to dry up soon," the crane said sadly.

Don't believe his story. He is our enemy.

All the fishes were filled with fear. But, there was one crab in the pond who did not believe the crane's story.

The foolish fishes did not listen to the crab. They asked the crane to help them escape from the pond.

So, the crane carried one fish to a distant lake and brought him back. When the fish told the others about how big and deep the lake was, they were all very anxious to leave their little pond and go there.

But, after that first time, the crane did not take the fishes to any lake. He flew away with the fishes all right, but only to a tree some way off. One after the other, he carried them to the tree. One after the other, he ate them up and threw the bones down.

When there were no fishes left in the pond, the crane offered to carry the crab to the lake. Since he was too big for the crane's beak, the crab held on to the crane's long neck with his strong claws.

"You wicked crane, you killed all my poor friends! Now it is your turn to die!"

Suddenly, the crab saw that the crane was flying towards a tree. At the bottom of the tree, there was a heap of fish bones. The crab realised that the crane had lured the poor fishes there and killed them. He pressed harder upon the neck of the crane that he was holding on to. Using his strong claws, the crab choked the wicked crane to death.

Moral: Evil to him that evil plots.

MEANINGS OF DIFFICULT WORDS

The Lion and the Talking Cave

prey	– target of an attack
lame	– with a defect in the leg
restless	– moving about or not content
impatient	– unwilling to wait
pugmarks	– foot prints of an animal

The Owl and the Swan

authority	– power or control
hooting	– call of an owl
omens	– signs of something about to happen
remorse	– regret or upset over something
vain	– proud

The Fox and the Grapes

vineyard	– place or garden where grapes are grown
ripe	– ready to eat
vines	– creeper or climbing plant
hedge	– small shrub or bush
despise	– hate or dislike

MEANINGS OF DIFFICULT WORDS

The Brahmin and His Foolish Sons

curious	– wanting to know more
similar	– alike
bound	– tied together

The Tree That Talked

hatching a plot	– making a plan
accused	– blamed of some wrong-doing
witness	– onlooker

The Brahmin and His Dream

alms	– aid or help given in the form of charity
pious	– god-fearing or religious

MEANINGS OF DIFFICULT WORDS

The Cap Seller and the Monkeys

scampered – ran off
imitated – repeated what someone else did

The Crow and the Jackal

cunning – sly
ignored – refused to notice
flattered – complimented excessively

The Crane and the Crab

anxious – worried
claws – nails of a bird or animal
lured – attracted
plots – makes a plan